GEORGIA

Karen Diane Haywood

Jessica Cohn

Cavendish
Square

New York

Published in 2014 by Cavendish Square Publishing, LLC
303 Park Avenue South, Suite 1247, New York, NY 10010

Website: cavendishsq.com

This publication represents the opinions and views of the author based on his or her personal experience, knowledge, and research. The information in this book serves as a general guide only. The author and publisher have used their best efforts in preparing this book and disclaim liability rising directly or indirectly from the use and application of this book.

CPSIA Compliance Information: Batch #WS13CSQ

All websites were available and accurate when this book was sent to press.

Library of Congress Cataloging-in-Publication Data
Haywood, Karen Diane.
      Georgia / Karen Diane Haywood and Jessica Cohn.—2nd ed.
         p. cm.—(It's my state!)
      Summary: "Surveys the history, geography, government, economy, and
      people of Georgia"—Provided by publisher.
      Includes blbiographical references and index.
      ISBN 978-1-60870-879-6 (hardcover)—ISBN 978-1-62712-092-0 (paperback)—ISBN 978-1-60870-885-7 (ebook)
      1. Georgia—Juvenile literature. I. Cohn, Jessica. II. Title.
  F286.3.H395 2013
  975.8—dc23   2012005164

This edition developed for Cavendish Square Publishing by RJF Publishing LLC (www.RJFpublishing.com)
Series Designer, Second Edition: Tammy West/Westgraphix LLC
Editor, Second Edition: Emily Dolbear

GEORGIA

CONTENTS

A Quick Look at
GEORGIA

State Tree: Live Oak

The live oak became the state tree in 1937. In Georgia, live oaks grow inland, along the coastal plain, and on the barrier islands. The largest live oak in the state, near Baptist Village in Waycross, stands 86 feet (26 meters) high. Its trunk is 10 feet (3 m) wide. With a limb spread of 143 feet (44 m), the large tree shades nearly 0.5 acre (0.2 hectares).

State Insect: Honeybee

Honeybees make a valuable contribution to Georgia's economy. In addition to producing honey, they cross-pollinate many crops. By naming the honeybee the state insect in 1975, officials recognized its importance to the state's agricultural interests.

State Bird: Brown Thrasher

The brown thrasher inspired the name of Georgia's first professional hockey team. The thrasher is about 1 foot (0.3 m) long. Its tail makes up nearly half its length. The thrasher feeds mainly on insects. The thrasher's name may have come from the way the bird tosses aside leaves with its beak while searching for food on the ground.

State Fish: Largemouth Bass

In 1970, Georgia's legislature made this bass the official state fish. It is the largest of black basses. Largemouth bass can weigh more than 12 pounds (5 kilograms) and grow longer than 25 inches (64 centimeters).

State Reptile: Gopher Tortoise

Designated the state reptile in 1989, the gopher tortoise is one of the oldest living species native to the state. Its population has declined, however. This special land tortoise is now listed as threatened—at risk of becoming endangered, which would put it in danger of dying out— in Georgia. It is illegal to keep one as a pet. In the wild, the gopher tortoise digs burrows up to 40 feet (12 m) wide and 10 feet (3 m) deep.

State Prepared Food: Grits

Grits became Georgia's official prepared food in 2002. Made of ground corn, grits are a traditional Southern food. Many people add meat, vegetables, fruit, seasonings, or sweeteners to this popular dish.

GEORGIA

BRASSTOW BALD

APPALACHIAN

Dalton

CHATTAHOOCHEE NATIONAL FOREST

APPALACHIAN TRAIL

BLUE RIDGE MOUNTAINS

Calhoun

Lake Lanier

Gainesville

Hartwell Lake

Rome

Russell Lake

Athens

Clarks Hill Lake

N

YELLOW RIVER

OCONEE NATIONAL FOREST

Atlanta

W   E

CHATTAHOOCHEE RIVER

Jackson Lake

OCONEE NATIONAL FOREST

Lake Oconee

Augusta

SAVANNAH RIVER

FLINT RIVER

OCMULGEE RIVER

Lake Sinclair

S

West Lake

Macon

Lake Harding

OCONEE RIVER

Columbus

Savannah

Walter F. George Lake

Lake Blackshear

ALTAMAHA RIVER

Hinesville

Albany

FLINT RIVER

BLACKBEARD ISLAND NATIONAL WILDLIFE REFUGE

GRAYS REEF NATIONAL MARINE SANCTUARY

CUMBERLAND ISLAND NATIONAL SEASHORE

Valdost

SUWANNEE

Okefenokee Swamp

ATLANTIC OCEAN

Lake Seminole

OKEFENOKEE NATIONAL WILDLIFE REFUGE

ST. MARY'S RIVER

The Peach State

Georgia's landscape offers a variety of geographic features, from the mountain peaks and canyons of the Appalachian Mountains in the north to the southern swamps and plains. The Peach State is divided into 159 counties and several distinctive land regions. In addition to its two most famous cities—historic Savannah and modern Atlanta—Georgia boasts stately plantation homes, historic small towns, the world's largest azalea garden, and the mysterious Okefenokee Swamp.

Georgia is the largest state east of the Mississippi River, in terms of land area. It covers 57,513 square miles (148,958 square kilometers). Mountains rim the north, coastal plains cover the south, and the central part of the state features rolling hills. The state has six main land regions. The Gulf Coastal Plain covers the southwest region, and the Atlantic Coastal Plain is in the southeast, reaching eastward to the Atlantic Ocean. The Blue Ridge Mountains (part of the Appalachians) are situated in the northeast. The Appalachian Plateau and the Appalachian Ridge and Valley region mark the northwestern corner. The Piedmont Plateau sweeps across the middle of the state.

Quick Facts

GEORGIA BORDERS

North	North Carolina
	Tennessee
South	Florida
East	South Carolina
	Atlantic Ocean
West	Alabama

DADE
CATOOSA
WHITFIELD
MURRAY
WALKER
FANNIN
TOWNS
RABUN
UNION
WHITE
HABER-SHAM
GILMER
LUMPKIN
STEPHENS
CHATTOOGA
GORDON
PICKENS
DAWSON
BANKS
FRANKLIN
HART
FLOYD
BARTOW
CHEROKEE
FORSYTH
HALL
JACKSON
MADISON
ELBERT
POLK
PAULDING
COBB
GWINNETT
BARROW
CLARKE
OCONEE
OGLETHORPE
WILKES
LINCOLN
HARALSON
DOUGLAS
FULTON
DE KALB
WALTON
ROCKDALE
MORGAN
GREENE
TALIAFERRO
COLUMBIA
McDUFFIE
CARROLL
CLAYTON
NEWTON
WARREN
RICHMOND
FAYETTE
HENRY
JASPER
PUTNAM
HANCOCK
GLASCOCK
HEARD
COWETA
SPALDING
BUTTS
BURKE
TROUP
MERIWETHER
PIKE
LAMAR
MONROE
JONES
BALDWIN
JEFFERSON
UPSON
WASHINGTON
HARRIS
TALBOT
CRAWFORD
BIBB
WILKINSON
JOHNSON
JENKINS
SCREVEN
MUSCOGEE
TWIGGS
EMANUEL
TAYLOR
PEACH
LAURENS
CHATTA-HOOCHEE
MARION
MACON
HOUSTON
BLECKLEY
TREUTLEN
CANDLER
BULLOCH
EFFINGHAM
SCHLEY
PULASKI
MONT-GOMERY
EVANS
STEWART
WEBSTER
SUMTER
DOOLY
DODGE
WHEELER
TOOMBS
TATTNALL
BRYAN
CHATHAM
QUITMAN
CRISP
WILCOX
TELFAIR
LIBERTY
RANDOLPH
TERRELL
LEE
TURNER
BEN HILL
JEFF DAVIS
APPLING
LONG
CLAY
CALHOUN
DOUGHERTY
WORTH
TIFT
IRWIN
COFFEE
BACON
WAYNE
McINTOSH
EARLY
BAKER
BERRIEN
ATKINSON
PIERCE
GLYNN
MILLER
MITCHELL
COLQUITT
COOK
WARE
BRANTLEY
SEMINOLE
LANIER
CHARLTON
CAMDEN
DECATUR
GRADY
THOMAS
BROOKS
LOWNDES
CLINCH
ECHOLS

Georgia has 159 counties.

Georgia and Tennessee share 40,000 acres (16,000 ha) of wilderness, called Cohutta on Georgia's side. In Tennessee, the same woods are called Big Frog.

The Northern Landscape

In northeastern Georgia, the Blue Ridge Mountains rise out of the broad valleys and forest-covered ridges of the foothills. Millions of people have explored this region by walking along the Appalachian National Scenic Trail. This famous footpath starts in Georgia at Springer Mountain and curves northward past Blood and Big Cedar mountains. It reaches north more than 2,000 miles (3,200 km) to Mount Katahdin in Maine.

The northwestern corner is part of the Appalachian Plateau, which extends from New York to Alabama. A plateau is a flat-topped portion of land that sits above the surrounding region. The plateau in Georgia was lifted upward during the time the Appalachians formed. Just south of this rugged surface is the Appalachian Ridge and Valley region, a belt of scenic mountains known for their even ridges and long valleys.

The Cohutta Wilderness, which Georgia shares with Tennessee, can also be found in the northwestern part of the state. Here, mountains house caves and canyons that have—so far—been largely unaffected by tourism and development.

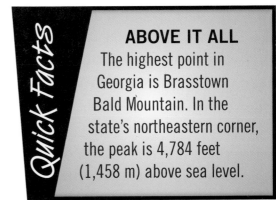

Quick Facts

ABOVE IT ALL
The highest point in Georgia is Brasstown Bald Mountain. In the state's northeastern corner, the peak is 4,784 feet (1,458 m) above sea level.

A carving on Stone Mountain, located near Atlanta, features leaders of the Confederacy during the Civil War.

The Piedmont

The state capital, Atlanta, is located on the Piedmont Plateau. This central region is characterized by gently rolling hills and red clay soil. Atlanta is about 50 miles (80 km) south of the Appalachians. However, the Atlanta area ranges in elevation from about 850 feet to 1,100 feet (260 m to 340 m) and has several mountains that rise 300 feet to 800 feet (90 m to 240 m) higher. Just east of Atlanta is Stone Mountain, a monstrous mound of gray rock 825 feet (251 m) tall.

At the western end of the Piedmont Plateau, Pine Mountain rises from the plains near Warm Springs. At 1,500 feet (460 m) in elevation, Pine Mountain is a popular area for Georgians to find relief from the summer heat and to soak in the heated mineral springs that flow from the mountainside.

The South

While the famous Georgia peach is grown mainly in the valleys of the Piedmont, the south is where peanuts, pecans, and a variety of other fruits and vegetables are grown. Sweet Vidalia onions, watermelons, soybeans, sweet potatoes,

Quick Facts

NO SMALL PEANUTS

It may be called the Peach State, but Georgia raises nearly half of another crop produced in the United States—the peanut. The state typically produces more than 1.5 million pounds (680,000 kg) of peanuts a year. In 2011, however, drought conditions decreased supply and increased the cost of peanut butter at the supermarket.

The state of Georgia grows more than forty varieties of peach.

The Okefenokee National Wildlife Refuge was created in 1937 to protect the area's plants and animals.

and sugarcane are harvested in the south's farms and orchards. Like the peach, the Vidalia onion is important to Georgia's identity and the state's farming history. It gets its name from a Vidalia farmers' market where the sweet onion first became popular.

Farther south, past the farms, the soil becomes sandier. On the southeastern edge of the region, just south of Waycross, is the Okefenokee Swamp. This nearly 700-square-mile (1,800-sq-km) wilderness of black water, once the home of the Seminole people, is now the site of a national wildlife refuge. *Oka* means "water," and *fenoke* means "shaking" in the Hitchiti language. Over time, *Okefenokee* has come to mean the "land of the trembling earth."

The area was once a large sandbar—a ridge of sand created by water currents—under the Atlantic Ocean. As the ocean retreated, some water remained trapped in a pool. The pool filled with rainwater and runoff water and became a freshwater lake over time. The freshwater became full of vegetation, such as dead leaves. As the vegetation decayed, the swamp was born. Although the swamp looks dark and dirty, it was formed by nature, and its water is safe for animals to drink.

Along the Atlantic coast, natural forces formed barrier islands and marshes. Barrier islands are long and narrow islands that are formed by waves, currents, and winds near a seashore. These kinds of islands, common on the Atlantic coast of North America, are rare throughout the rest of the world. Barrier island chains lie along only 2.2 percent of the world's coastlines.

Sixty million years ago, southern Georgia was underwater. Today, miners often find fossilized bones of prehistoric whales, sharks, and other marine creatures. The towns of Savannah, Darien, and Brunswick are built on land that was a string of barrier islands during ancient times. The islands formed when the sea level was 15 feet to 25 feet (5 m to 8 m) higher than it is now. As the water receded, the coastline moved eastward.

Georgia's coast has changed dramatically over the ages. Around 18,000 years ago, during the last Ice Age, the sea level was 400 feet (120 m) lower, and the coastline was 95 miles (153 km) east of where it is now. Along the Atlantic coast, nature's handiwork is still not done. The winds and tides are making constant revisions.

The Waterways

Georgia's Atlantic coast is more than 100 miles (160 km) long. When sea levels rose, sand dunes along the shoreline became islands and the protected areas between the islands and the mainland became lagoons. These lagoons eventually developed into the salt marshes of Georgia. Crabs, oysters, mussels, and shrimp populate these marshes, but few plants except for tall grass survive.

The marshes form a long waterway known as the Inland Passage. This water highway is protected from the wilder weather out on the Atlantic, making it possible for small boats to move along the coast even during storms at sea. Only a couple of areas along the Inland Passage are problematic for sea travel. These shallow spots are known as the narrows. At times, it is necessary to dredge them.

Canoes travel through the long waterway known as the Inland Passage.

Dredging is the process of gathering materials from the bottom of the water and moving them elsewhere, so that the water becomes deeper.

The major rivers in Georgia are the Chattahoochee, the Savannah, and the Suwannee. The first two start in northeastern Georgia. The Chattahoochee joins other rivers in the south, and its waters eventually flow into the Gulf of Mexico. The Savannah flows into the Atlantic. The Suwannee begins in the southeast. It flows through the Okefenokee Swamp and northern Florida to the Gulf of Mexico. There are many other, smaller rivers throughout the state.

Along the southern edge of the Piedmont Plateau is a natural boundary called the fall line. Waterfalls occur along the fall line, as river waters spill over the end of the higher plateau onto lower land. In Georgia, where early commerce relied on using the rivers to transport goods and people, cities emerged at the fall line, where ships could go no farther inland. Augusta was built at the fall line of the Savannah River. Columbus is found on the Chattahoochee fall line.

Waterfalls grace more than thirty spots in the state. The captivating waterfalls in northwestern Georgia include the double falls in Cloudland Canyon State Park. Amicalola Falls near Dawsonville are the state's tallest falls.

The state has both natural and human-made lakes. Human-made lakes are created by engineers to store water, help control floods, generate electricity, and offer recreation. The Great Lakes of Georgia are nine such lakes. Many of the larger human-made lakes are in the northern part of the state, where the land is mountainous.

Climate

Georgia spans so much land that the daily weather varies depending on the region. The weather is affected by altitude, or how high an area sits above sea level. It is also dependent on how close or far an area is to the ocean. However, for the most part, the state has mild winters and hot summers.

Georgians experience a range of seasonal changes no matter where they live—though some of these changes are more dramatic than others. The trees of northwestern Georgia showcase colorful leaves in autumn. It is usually milder

While summers are hot in Georgia, Atlanta residents find a recreational oasis at Piedmont Park.

in the Piedmont than in the northern mountains. In the Piedmont, snow is rare in the winter, and the summers are very hot and humid, with frequent thunderstorms.

In the Okefenokee Swamp, the weather is mild in the spring and fall, but hot and humid in the summer. Winter temperatures vary between cool and hot in the daytime, occasionally going down to freezing at night.

The climate along the Atlantic is generally mild, with hot summers and cool winters. Precipitation, which is the amount of water that falls as rain or snow, is high. During summer, however, a high-pressure system called the Bermuda High settles in the southeast, and its winds affect the weather. The Bermuda High produces occasional droughts, or long periods without rain.

Nature's extremes are also on display where the North American coastline tucks inward, between Cape Hatteras in North Carolina and Cape Canaveral in Florida. This area, where the tides are particularly strong, is called the Georgia Bight. In some years, one or more hurricanes hit the coast. With winds up to 200 miles (320 km) an hour, these storms can be devastating. The Georgia coast has a 5 percent risk of hurricanes each year. August, September, and October are the most common months for the storms.

Wildlife

Georgia has hundreds of thousands of plant and animal species. Because the state is made up of such diverse regions, many types of trees grow well in

About 200,000 American alligators live in Georgia.

Georgia. Birch, cedar, beech, and hickory trees are found in the state, as well as palmetto, oak, maple, and poplar varieties. The trees and other plants provide shelter and food for a wide range of Georgia's wildlife.

Bears, beaver, snakes, deer, foxes, and raccoons make their homes in forests, fields, and wetlands. Amphibians such as salamanders, frogs, and toads live in watery areas. Alligators swim in the shallow waters of the Okefenokee Swamp. Lake Seminole is a 12,000-acre (4,900-ha) lake filled with bass. Largemouth, scrappy hybrid, striped, and white bass swim with catfish, crappie, and bream. In some parts of Georgia, as is true of many areas in the Southeast, wild boars run free.

Birdwatchers spot cardinals, robins, blue jays, catbirds, larks, and wrens in Georgia skies. On the ground, feathered species such as herons, egrets, and cranes search for food in the water.

In the Okefenokee Swamp, cypress trees draped with Spanish moss tower over the water lilies floating on the water. The fly-eating pitcher plant grows below the trees, as hummingbirds and whooping cranes fly above.

Each year, more than ninety species of birds, including whooping cranes, stop or stay in Georgia as they migrate southward.

Endangered Wildlife

One challenge facing Georgians is the introduction of exotic, or non-native, species to their natural areas. When non-native plants such as kudzu, wisteria, English ivy, and bamboo take over, they destroy native plants. Fast-growing kudzu from China and Japan, for example, is disrupting the growth of native plants throughout the Southeast.

The same is true for invasive animals. European starlings were introduced in New York in 1890, and they have since spread as far south as Georgia. Starlings and house sparrows, which were brought from Britain in the 1850s to help rid shade trees of inchworms, now compete with native species for food and places to nest. Fire ants were introduced in the South in the 1930s after cargo ships unintentionally transported them from Brazil. Now, they damage crops and electrical equipment throughout the state.

However, the greatest problem facing Georgia wildlife is loss of habitat, as the population increases and more land becomes developed

Kudzu, introduced to control erosion, has since earned the nickname the Plant That Ate the South.

Florida panthers, which once roamed the Southeast, are now considered rare.

for homes and businesses. Shrinking habitats cause a decrease in species numbers and a loss in species variety. Clearing trees destroys animal homes and exposes the ground to more sunlight and drier conditions. This exposure can kill other plants and animals. Removing the understory (the layer of plants that grows beneath the tallest trees) exposes small animals to birds and larger animals that will kill them for food. Destroying understory also affects the animals' nests, shelter, and sources of food.

Concerned scientists and residents have worked together to protect the state's wildlife. Laws have been passed to prevent the harming of certain animals, including the Florida panther and the leatherback sea turtle. Special portions of land and water have been set aside and protected so that the native species can thrive away from humans. Pollution is controlled by laws and regulations. Knowing that their land—and all the life growing upon it—is very valuable, Georgians do what they can to protect and treasure it.

Plants & Animals

Nutria

The nutria is a large rodent that lives near water and eats plants and roots. Adult nutrias can weigh up to 12 pounds (5 kg) and can grow to be around 2 feet (0.6 m) long. They can swim long distances underwater. In the past, nutrias were hunted for their fur, which was used for hats and clothing.

Manatee

Manatees are gentle sea mammals found in Georgia's coastal waters. These huge creatures can weigh more than 2,000 pounds (900 kg). They eat mainly sea grass and other plants. Because there are so few manatees in the wild, they are considered endangered. It is illegal to harass, hunt, or kill them. Boaters must take care to avoid hitting these endangered animals.

Bald Cypress

The bald cypress tree grows in swamps and along rivers, lakes, and stream banks throughout the Coastal Plain along the Atlantic. A variety of waterfowl and marsh birds eats the seeds of these trees. Eagles, ospreys, and herons often nest in the branches.

Barking Tree Frog

Barking tree frogs can grow to be about 3 inches (8 cm) in length. The barking tree frog is nocturnal, which means that it rests during the day and moves around and eats at night. These frogs live throughout much of Georgia. The noise that they make sounds like a barking dog.

Mountain Laurel

The mountain laurel is found on rocky slopes and stream banks in the Piedmont, the mountains, and the Atlantic Coastal Plain. Besides being beautiful to look at, the plant provides food and shelter for many birds and small animals.

Azalea

In 1979, the azalea was chosen as Georgia's state wildflower. Many types of azalea grow across the state. A hardy plant, the azalea has vibrantly colored blossoms that usually bloom between March and August.

From the Beginning

Georgia's written history begins with the Spanish explorers of the mid-sixteenth century. Its unwritten history goes back thousands of years. Prehistoric hunters moved into the region about 12,000 years ago. Little is known about them, but their descendants left evidence of their cultures.

Thousands of years ago, people now referred to as the Mound Builders prospered in the area. The name of this early American Indian culture describes the people's settlements, which featured great earthen mounds. These structures have been found in locations from the Great Lakes to the Gulf of Mexico, on the land between the Mississippi River and the Appalachian Mountains.

The Mound Builders lived in what is now Georgia about 3,000 to 1,500 years ago. They constructed the Kolomoki Mounds, near Blakely. The site is one of the largest complexes of mounds in the area, but many other sites also serve as reminders of the time when American Indians were the only inhabitants in the area. The Rock Eagle Effigy Mound stands near Eatonton. The Ocmulgee National Monument is the site of ancient mounds in Macon.

Quick Facts

FORM AND FUNCTION

The mounds of the Mound Builders seemed to serve a variety of functions. Some were burial mounds. Others seem to have been platforms used for religious ceremonies.

Rock Eagle Effigy Mound is an ancient mound of rocks in the shape of a giant eagle.

The Etowah Indian Mounds Historic Site features six earthen mounds built by an ancient society.

The mound-building Mississippian culture flourished from about 850 CE until the arrival of European explorers. It is clear from their artifacts, such as pottery, that these people were skilled craftspeople with a complex system of trading. The most well-preserved Mississippian cultural site in the East is Georgia's Etowah Indian Mounds near Cartersville.

By the time the Spanish explorer Hernando de Soto arrived in 1540, the Mississippian culture was in decline, and the Etowah Mounds site had been abandoned. However, there was still a strong American Indian presence in Georgia. A large portion of the American Indian population was destroyed by de Soto's expedition and the Spanish settlers who followed. Spanish soldiers killed or kidnapped many of the American Indians, forcing the survivors into slavery. European diseases wiped out many of the others.

Those who survived the arrival of the Spanish retreated to remote areas of the region. They became known as the Cherokee and Creek nations. The Cherokee, whose territory reached into what is now the Carolinas and Virginia, lived in

Cherokee Indians constructed different types of shelter, including small houses of mud and clay over woven branches.

the mountains of today's northern Georgia. The Creek Nation, also called the Muscogee, later became known as the Creek Confederacy. These people lived in the eastern part of present-day Georgia.

The Europeans

In 1562, France tried to establish a colony in Port Royal Sound, with the help of the American Indians. The arrival of the French alarmed the Spanish, and in 1565, Spanish troops attacked and killed the French settlers. Soon after, the Spanish built a fort on St. Catherines Island. From there, Spanish priests set out to convert the American Indians to Christianity. Their missions, or religious settlements, were the first European settlements on the Georgia mainland.

Indian populations in the area began to decline. There were also Indian and pirate attacks on some of the missions. By the end of the 1600s, all the missions had been abandoned and there were virtually no Spanish settlements north of Florida.

In the early 1700s, the number of Europeans living in what is now Georgia was relatively small. This changed after the British arrived, however. The British had already colonized the coast farther north. In 1732, King George II of Great

James Oglethorpe founded the colony of Georgia and served as its first governor.

Britain sent General James Oglethorpe to create a new colony near Spanish Florida, as a means of defense.

The first boatload of British settlers, led by Oglethorpe, landed in 1733. They named the area Georgia after their king and called their settlement Savannah. The Spanish invaded Georgia and attacked the English in 1742. After losing the battle, the Spanish retreated to Saint Augustine, in Florida, and did not return.

With the British came enslaved African Americans. At first, Oglethorpe banned slavery in Savannah. But before long, British immigrants were renting slaves from South Carolina. Other British settlers in Virginia and the Carolinas used slave labor to grow valuable crops such as rice and indigo, a plant used to make colorful dye. Georgia's ban was eventually abandoned.

By 1760, thousands of slaves had been brought into Georgia to work in the fields. Their forced labor made it possible for Sea Island cotton to prosper along the coast. Rice plantations spread up the Savannah River and down the Atlantic Coastal Plain.

The American Revolution

In the 1760s, Great Britain began to enforce new policies in the American colonies. It imposed new taxes and restrictions on colonial trade that many colonists resented. In addition, some of the British representatives sent to oversee the colonists were of questionable character and not always appointed on merit, which made matters worse.

However, Georgia was the youngest colony, and many of its citizens had been born in Britain. Their ties to their "homeland" were stronger than those of people in most other colonies. When the First Continental Congress was held in Philadelphia in 1774 to discuss how the colonies should respond to British policies, twelve of the thirteen colonies that would become the United States sent delegates. Georgia was the one colony that sent no delegates. The Second Continental Congress began soon after the start of the American Revolution in the spring of 1775. At first, only one delegate from one part of Georgia showed up. But by 1776, Georgia was one of the thirteen colonies that declared independence from Britain.

In the fighting that followed, the British captured the port of Savannah, and by 1779, most of Georgia was officially under British control. Yet intense fighting raged in the Georgia-Carolina backcountry. As much as half of the property in Georgia was destroyed by 1783, when the American Revolution ended and Britain recognized American independence. The area recovered quickly when the fighting was finally finished, however.

Georgia officially became a state on January 2, 1788, when it ratified the U.S. Constitution. With a new wave of immigration from other states and from overseas, the population in 1790 was more than double what it had been at the beginning of the war.

MAKING A SILHOUETTE

Before cameras were invented, people captured images of other people by sketching, drawing, or painting them. In colonial times, the silhouette became a popular way to display the outline of a person's features with cut paper. Here are simple instructions for creating an old-fashioned silhouette, using modern craft materials.

WHAT YOU NEED

A partner

A large piece of white paper, at least $8\frac{1}{2}$ inches by 11 inches (22 cm by 28 cm)

Cellophane tape

A flashlight

A pencil

Scissors

Construction paper

Paste

Have your partner stand sideways about 1 foot (30 cm) away from a wall. The wall should be at his or her side. Tape the white paper on the wall at the height of your partner's head.

Take several steps back from your partner and set up the flashlight with the light directed toward his or her head. You can place the flashlight on a table, a chair, a box, or a pile of books.

The light from the flashlight should create a shadow on the paper on the wall. Using the pencil, trace the outline of the shadow. Be careful not to draw on the wall.

Take the paper down and cut along the outline of your partner's profile. Then paste the cutout on the construction paper.

To make a more colorful silhouette, place the cutout on construction paper, trace the outline, and cut out a colored version. Paste this colored version onto another piece of paper. Or you may prefer a black cutout on white paper. Many people like the look of black-on-white silhouettes because they seem like real shadows.

Switch places with your partner and repeat the process. Paste your silhouette on a separate sheet of construction paper, or paste the two images side by side.

Decorate the borders as desired. For example, you may want to write your names and the date. Now, your works of art are ready for display.

The 1800s Begin

Before the American Revolution, the British and the American Indians in Georgia struggled for control of land. After American independence, Georgia farmers moved west into the tribal lands of the Cherokee and the Creek. In 1811, a council of Creek chiefs tried to prevent further land sales to the U.S. settlers. But they were unable to enforce their will, and by 1827, most of the Creek were removed to Oklahoma.

Many of the Cherokee followed the Creek. Those that remained suffered through a forced migration, ordered by the U.S. government, called the Trail of Tears. In 1838, U.S. general Winfield Scott and his troops rounded up the 14,000 Cherokee who were still in Georgia, along with those from the Carolinas. The soldiers forced the American Indians to march to Indian Territory, in what is now Oklahoma. It took the Cherokee more than five months to walk the more than 1,000 miles (1,600 km) in freezing winter weather. One-third of the prisoners died from the harsh conditions.

Cold weather, a lack of food, and poor treatment from U.S. troops led to the death of thousands of Cherokee Indians during the Trail of Tears.

The land taken from the Indians was given over to the pursuit of profits. In 1790, several years after the end of the American Revolution, farmers in Georgia grew only 1,000 bales of cotton. By 1820, Georgia's plantations were harvesting 90,000 bales of cotton each year. By 1860, before the start of the Civil War (1861–1865), the number of bales had surpassed 700,000.

The rapid growth of the cotton industry was largely due to slave labor. By 1860, Georgia had about 465,000 African-American slaves, working in the fields and their owners' homes. Though there were exceptions, many slaves suffered terrible punishments and endured harsh living conditions. The plantation workers lived with little or no medical care.

In 1829, because of fear of slave uprisings, the state legislature made it illegal for anyone to teach African Americans to read or write. By 1833, slaves could not own property, testify against whites in court, travel without a special pass, bear weapons, or work in printing shops. There was no such thing as a legal slave marriage or family. Slaves were considered the property of their owners, who could break up slave families and sell family members separately. Only by a special act of the legislature could a slave gain freedom. Harsh laws were passed to keep the few African Americans who were freed from prospering.

The rich plantation owners exerted wide influence. According to the U.S. Census of 1860, twenty-three planters owned more than two hundred slaves each. Less than one percent of the state's white population was in the planter class, defined as men owning more than twenty slaves. Most white Georgians were self-supporting small farmers. Some of them lived well. But others, particularly those living in the northern hill country, found it a challenge to put food on the table. Cotton profits were so important to the state, however, that a small group of large-scale planters and slave owners dominated the state government.

The Civil War

Slavery, and the treatment of the slaves, became a wedge between the states of the North and the South. In the industrial economy of the North, poor

At the start of the Civil War, slaves were 44 percent of the population of Georgia.

immigrants from overseas provided affordable labor in the region's growing number of factories. By the mid-1800s, slavery had been outlawed in most Northern states. However, the South had fewer people and far less industry. The success of the Southern economy relied on growing cotton, as well as other crops such as rice and tobacco, on plantations, which depended on the labor of slaves.

In the U.S. Congress, Representative Alexander H. Stephens of Georgia worked with Northern congressmen to create the Compromise of 1850. This set of laws kept the peace between the North and South for ten years. However, the issue of slavery had to be addressed as the United States expanded into the West. The federal government needed to determine whether slavery would be legal in western territories.

During the 1860 presidential election campaign, Abraham Lincoln opposed slavery in the West. When Lincoln was elected in November, Southern officials felt threatened. Southern states began to secede, or withdraw, from the Union (another term used for the United States at that time). South Carolina seceded in December. Georgia followed in January 1861.

In April 1861, war broke out between the North and South, and Georgia's young men crowded the recruiting offices to join the army of the new Confederate States of America. By 1862, Georgia troop totals reached 75,000. The state's factories and workshops in Macon, Columbus, Savannah, Dalton, Rome, Athens, and Augusta produced cannons, firearms, ammunition, clothing, and other gear for the soldiers.

Georgia's ports and rail lines became major Union targets. In the spring of 1862, the Union navy landed on Tybee Island at the mouth of the Savannah River. On the morning of April 10, Union cannons fired on the walls of Fort Pulaski. The Union navy closed the port of Savannah to ships carrying much-needed food and supplies to the South. The Union army concentrated on destroying the rails. By 1860, Georgia had about 1,200 miles (1,930 km) of railroad track—more than any other Southern state. The Union strategy was to close off supplies by destroying the transportation system.

In the fall of 1863, Union troops under Major General William Rosecrans captured Chattanooga, Tennessee, and then moved into northwest Georgia. A Confederate force under Major General Braxton Bragg met them along the banks of Chickamauga Creek. In a fierce two-day battle, 34,700 Union and Confederate soldiers were killed or wounded. The Union army retreated northward, but the battle was just a preview of the action to come.

In May 1864, Union general William Tecumseh Sherman marched into Georgia with nearly 100,000 soldiers. Their mission was to seize Atlanta and cripple the Confederate war effort. The troops of Confederate general Joseph E. Johnston were able to slow but not stop Sherman's advance. Outside Atlanta, Confederate general John Bell Hood, who replaced Johnston, managed to hold the city for forty days, but Union forces gained the upper hand. On September 2, Sherman's troops entered the city.

In mid-November, Sherman left Atlanta in flames and began his infamous March to the Sea. Sherman and his troops marched toward the Atlantic coast, creating a trail of destruction approximately 50 miles (80 km) wide. Farms and plantations were burned, livestock were slaughtered, and private property was

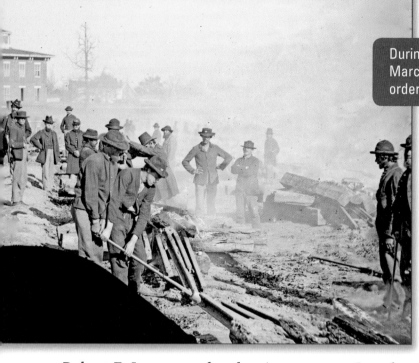

During the burning of Atlanta and the March to the Sea, Union troops were ordered to take apart railroad tracks.

stolen. Railroad tracks, bridges, factories, and mills were destroyed. The Union soldiers reached Savannah on December 21. The port city fell quickly.

On April 9, 1865, Confederate commander Robert E. Lee surrendered at Appomattox Courthouse, Virginia, in effect ending the Civil War. A month later, Union cavalry captured the Confederate president, Jefferson Davis, near Irwinville in southern Georgia.

The End of the 1800s

After the Civil War, hunger and disease ravaged the region. Georgia's war survivors struggled to make a living. To keep the peace, the U.S. government began a military occupation. Georgia was governed as part of a military district that also included Florida and Alabama.

During the period of rebuilding that followed, called Reconstruction, Georgia's former slaves—now freed—were given access to courts, the right to own property, and the right to make contracts. Some moved into Georgia's cities, while some stayed on the plantations where they had worked as slaves.

Even with greater freedoms, Georgia's African-American citizens did not enjoy much progress in day-to-day living. They were not, for example, allowed to testify against white Americans. By the 1870s, U.S. occupation troops were being withdrawn from the Southern states, and white Georgians gained control of the new state government. Georgia's legislators voted to make segregation—the separation of whites and blacks—a matter of law. African American and white Georgians lived separately and used separate public facilities.

Economics also held back African Americans. The sharecropping system of farming came into wide use during Reconstruction. In this system, poor families, black and white alike, farmed land owned by someone else, to whom they paid a large share of the harvest as rent. At the same time, the farmer had to buy seeds, farming supplies, tools, livestock, and groceries from the landowner. Under this system, it was difficult for a sharecropper to make a good living under the best of circumstances. A bad crop year meant financial disaster.

Two African-American colleges—Atlanta University and Morehouse College—opened soon after the war. However, there were few educational opportunities for younger African Americans. The public school system, established in 1871, had one system for white children and another for black children. The basic school law called for the two systems to be "equal so far as practicable." Although none of the public schools were very good in these early days, over the decades that Georgia and other Southern states had separate school systems for white and black students, the schools for blacks were generally of lower quality than the schools for whites.

Since its founding in 1867, Morehouse College, a private liberal arts college in Atlanta, has educated thousands of men.

Tenant farmers of any race in Georgia had trouble getting an education in the late 1800s and early 1900s. This group included anyone who rented land for growing crops. Agreements with their landowners ranged from sharecropping to much

fairer setups, but most land rentals guaranteed a hard life for farmers and their families. The tenants living in the poor northern counties had little or no access to schools.

To help educate the local impoverished children, Martha McChesney Berry, the daughter of landowners in Rome, opened her own schools in the hills and

In her later years, Martha McChesney Berry, who never attended college, received honorary doctorates from eight colleges and universities for her contributions to education.

mountains. She began by offering a Bible school in an abandoned church. In 1902, Berry used her 83 acres (34 ha) of land in Floyd County to build a boys' school. In 1909, she opened a girls' school. By 1926, the school had grown into a junior college, and it became a four-year college, Berry College, in 1932.

The 1900s Begin

Between the Civil War and World War II (1939–1945), regional and individual fortunes rose and fell. Between 1900 and 1916, the value of Georgia's cotton crop tripled. When the United States entered World War I (1914–1918) in 1917, Georgia's economy received a further boost. Savannah became a major shipbuilding center, and factories in many other cities produced large quantities of war material. The period of prosperity ended in 1920. The price of cotton dropped from 35 cents a pound (0.4 kg) in 1919 to 17 cents in 1920. Then, the fields were invaded by boll weevils, insects that eat away at the boll, or fiber, of cotton plants. Hungry boll weevils moved into Georgia after eating through crops in Texas, Mississippi, and Alabama. The Southern states that were dependent on cotton were hit hard.

In 1929, while Georgians were still contending with the fall of cotton prices and the boll weevil invasion, the New York Stock Exchange crashed. Within two years, the entire country fell into a deep economic slump called the Great Depression. For the first time since the 1890s, the price of cotton fell to 5 cents per pound (0.4 kg). Many Georgians had to give up farming and leave their land. Some relocated to other states to find employment. Those who stayed struggled to make ends meet.

Quick Facts

UNION MEMBERS
With long hours, challenging conditions, and poor pay, factory work was a rough way to earn a living in the early twentieth century. While workers in the North were protected by labor unions, their counterparts in the South had few protections. At the time of the Great Depression, only 3.2 percent of Georgia's industrial workers belonged to unions.

For many, the only available jobs were in the state's textile mills, which turned cotton into cloth. At the turn of the century, many northeastern textile manufacturers had moved their mills to the South, where workers earned less money and had longer working hours. Working conditions in the mills became so bad that mill workers agreed to a general strike across the Southern states. They walked out of their jobs in protest in early September 1934. By the end of the second week of the strike, about 44,000 out of a workforce of 60,000 people had walked out in Georgia. The Crown Cotton Mill in Dalton closed while textile workers joined craft workers in a parade of 1,500 marchers, extending over eight city blocks.

The governors of North Carolina and South Carolina called out the National Guard to stop the strikes and force workers back into their jobs. But the governor of Georgia, Eugene Talmadge, went one step further and declared a state of martial law. Military forces usually administer martial law in an emergency to maintain public order and safety. In Georgia, the National Guard arrested sixteen women and more than one hundred men near Newnan and imprisoned them at Fort McPherson near Atlanta.

Talmadge was a forceful man. When a public board refused to lower utility rates, he appointed a new board. During his time in office, he resisted racial integration and civil rights for African Americans. He opposed President Franklin Delano Roosevelt and his New Deal programs aimed at helping the poor and the jobless. Voted out of office in 1936, Talmadge was replaced by Eurith D. "Ed" Rivers.

With the U.S. entry into World War II in 1941, Georgia's economy improved, along with that of the rest of the nation. Government orders for military supplies rushed into the state's mills, factories, and shipyards. Bell Aircraft built a big factory in Marietta.

The recovery came with a human cost, however. About 320,000 men and women from Georgia were in uniform during the four years the United States was in the war. Of that number, 6,754 lost their lives defending their country.

The 1900s End

After the war ended in 1945, the South's industrial base expanded rapidly. Ford and General Motors built automobile plants in Georgia. Bell Aircraft reopened as Lockheed-Georgia. In order to work in the new factories, many Georgians left their farms and moved to the state's cities or even to other states. The middle class of workers grew stronger as jobs became more plentiful.

In this era of social change, the civil rights movement gained momentum. African Americans and others spoke out in favor of desegregation and equal opportunity. In the famous 1954 case *Brown v. Board of Education*, the U.S. Supreme Court ruled that segregation in public schools was unconstitutional. The Court required that all states integrate their school systems "with all deliberate speed."

The leaders of the civil rights movement included Martin Luther King Jr., a native of Georgia. In August 1963, civil rights groups held a march and rally in Washington, D.C., where King gave his now-famous "I Have a Dream" speech, expressing his hopes that all Americans could enjoy equal rights and equal treatment. The following

Martin Luther King Jr. (center) grew up in Atlanta, near the church where his grandfather served as pastor.

year, with the support of President Lyndon B. Johnson, Congress passed the first civil rights legislation since 1875.

By the late 1960s, Georgia had still not complied with the Supreme Court's 1954 ruling, and Georgia's schools became a flash point for the civil rights movement. King was serving as a pastor at the Ebenezer Baptist Church in Atlanta and as president of the Southern Christian Leadership Conference (SCLC), an organization working for equal rights. Through his sermons and speeches, he challenged the lack of progress. By leading marches and demonstrations, King used nonviolent protest to help make changes happen.

King was assassinated in Memphis, Tennessee, in 1968. Georgia's schools were not fully integrated until the early 1970s, but King's legacy lives on. The Martin Luther King Jr. Center for Nonviolent Social Change continues his work in Atlanta. In 2011, a national monument in King's honor was opened on the National Mall in Washington, D.C.

In 1972, Andrew Young became the first African-American member of Congress since Reconstruction. In 1973, when Maynard Jackson was elected the first African-American mayor of Atlanta, he also became the first African-American mayor of a large Southern city.

In 1976, Jimmy Carter, from Plains, was elected the first U.S. president from Georgia. A former naval officer, peanut farmer, and businessman, Carter went to the White House after serving as governor. After leaving the White House, Carter became one of the country's most active and involved former presidents. On December 10, 2002, Carter received the Nobel Peace Prize for decades of work for peace, democracy, and human rights.

Georgia Today

In recent decades, Georgia's history has been forged by businesses and those who run them. Coca-Cola, UPS, the Home Depot, and Georgia-Pacific are among the many big-name companies now based in the state. Since the late 1960s, Atlanta has been the financial and industrial capital of the South.

New South is a term used to emphasize the change from the slave-driven economy of Civil War times to today's economy, which is based on high-tech industry. The New South is a center for modern service industries, such as finance, and for technological advancements.

Atlanta, the capital of Georgia, is also the largest center of trade and industry in the southeastern United States.

Tyler Perry, who lives in Atlanta, became the highest-paid male entertainer in 2011.

As of the 2010 Census, 420,003 people were living in the city of Atlanta. The number of people living in Atlanta's metropolitan area, including Sandy Springs and Marietta, is far greater, however. This area is home to 5,268,860 people—more than half the state's population. Atlanta is a major transportation center, the headquarters of the U.S. Centers for Disease Control and Prevention, and a key communications center.

Businessman Ted Turner has built a large media, sports, and business empire in the city. After founding the Turner Communications Group, Ted Turner purchased the Atlanta Braves baseball team and began broadcasting a "superstation" from Atlanta. In 1980, he started the Cable News Network (CNN), a 24-hour all-news cable channel. Entertainment mogul Tyler Perry keeps his base of operations in the state.

Downtown Atlanta and its skyline have undergone dramatic changes since the 1970s. After the 1996 Summer Olympic Games were held in Atlanta, the most visible reminder was the new Centennial Olympic Park. In 2007, the World of Coca-Cola opened. It welcomes more than one million visitors each year.

But Georgia, of course, is much bigger than Atlanta. The cities of Augusta, Columbus, and Savannah and the county of Athens-Clark each have more than 100,000 residents. Many of Georgia's other towns have kept their down-home nature while sharing in the years of statewide economic growth. The people of Georgia support a thriving arts scene, from the symphony, ballet, and theater of the cities to the community arts councils and music venues of the smaller towns.

Important Dates

★ **c. 1000** BCE The Mound Builders begin living in what is now Georgia.

★ **850** CE The Mississippian culture begins to flourish in the region.

★ **1540** Spanish explorer Hernando de Soto travels through today's Georgia.

★ **1733** British general James Oglethorpe lands at Yamacraw Bluff and establishes the Georgia colony.

★ **1776** Georgia joins twelve other colonies in declaring independence from Great Britain.

★ **1788** Georgia is the fourth state to ratify the U.S. Constitution.

★ **1828** The first American Indian newspaper, *The Cherokee Phoenix*, is published in New Echota.

★ **1838** Thousands of Cherokee Indians are forced out of Georgia during the Trail of Tears.

★ **1861** Georgia secedes from the Union and joins the Confederacy.

★ **1864** Union general William Tecumseh Sherman captures Atlanta and marches to the sea.

★ **1866** Georgia becomes the first state to grant full property rights to married women.

★ **1937** Margaret Mitchell of Atlanta wins the Pulitzer Prize for her novel *Gone with the Wind*.

★ **1943** Georgia is the first state to lower the legal voting age from twenty-one to eighteen.

★ **1973** Atlanta becomes the first major Southern city to elect an African-American mayor, Maynard Jackson.

★ **1976** Jimmy Carter wins election as the thirty-ninth U.S. president and the first president born in Georgia.

★ **1996** The city of Atlanta hosts the Summer Olympics.

★ **2001** Shirley Franklin is elected the first female mayor of Atlanta and becomes the first black woman to lead a major Southern city.

★ **2002** Former U.S. president Jimmy Carter wins the Nobel Peace Prize.

★ **2010** According to the 2010 Census, Georgia gains 1.5 million people since 2000.

The People

From historic Savannah, Augusta, and Darien to the modern Atlanta metropolitan area, Georgia is a state of contrasts, especially between the old and the new. Some families can trace their ancestors back to the original colonists. Others have recently moved to Georgia but already call the Peach State home. In fact, many people fall into this second category. New residents with new dreams are constantly showing up in Georgia. It is now the ninth-most-populous state in the nation. The number of residents has just about doubled since 1970.

The First Residents

Georgia's first inhabitants were American Indians. Though the government forced many Indians out of the state in the decades after the American Revolution, some have returned or stayed in remote areas. They tried to maintain their traditional ways of life. Today, Georgia's American Indians represent less than one percent of the population. They include the Cherokee, the Creek—also known as the Muscogee—and the Hitchiti, Oconee, and Miccosukee.

When American Indians were being chased from the state, members of the Georgia Tribe of Eastern Cherokee, also called the Georgia Cherokees, remained in the northern counties. The site of the last Cherokee capital, New Echota, is located in northern Georgia. Today, American Indians live in numerous

Some Georgia residents can trace their roots back hundreds of years. British colonists settled Brunswick, with its waterfront and shrimp boats, in 1738.

Georgia's powwows feature dance and drumming performances.

towns and cities, attending schools, working in businesses, and playing a role in government. Some are trying to revive American Indian communities by building new settlements. In 2011, a group of Creek Indians asked the U.S. government to recognize land on the Georgia coast as a reservation.

The Early Settlers

In the early 1700s, British settlers, some with African-American slaves, lived along the Savannah River. In 1752, there were about 3,500 European settlers and 500 African Americans. When the British relaxed rules about land ownership, additional settlers and slaves arrived. In 1773, there were 33,000 people, half of whom were African American.

American Indians controlled the lands east and west of the river until after the American Revolution. After the war, greater numbers of settlers started spreading throughout the region, taking advantage of free land. This settlement forced the American Indians farther west.

Many poor European immigrants or their descendants who traveled to Georgia struggled to survive in the backwoods. Of the 53,897 farms in Georgia in 1860, right before the start of the Civil War, only 902 were larger than 1,000 acres (400 ha).

The Civil War brought great destruction to farms in Georgia. Farmers tried to restore their businesses and profits during the Reconstruction period but had limited success. After the slaves were freed, plantation owners were left without money or labor. At this time, many of these landowners entered agreements with tenant farmers.

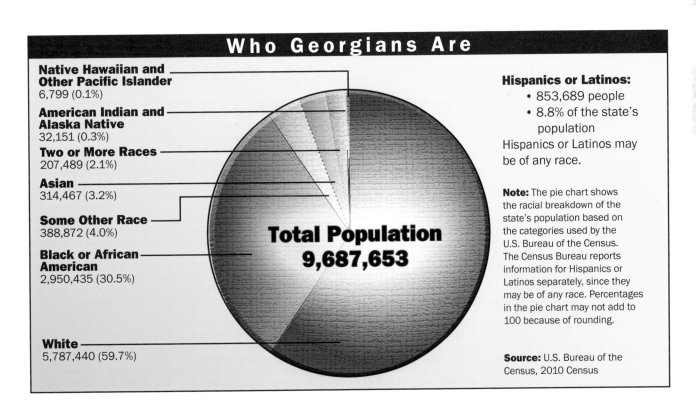

Who Georgians Are

Native Hawaiian and Other Pacific Islander
6,799 (0.1%)

American Indian and Alaska Native
32,151 (0.3%)

Two or More Races
207,489 (2.1%)

Asian
314,467 (3.2%)

Some Other Race
388,872 (4.0%)

Black or African American
2,950,435 (30.5%)

White
5,787,440 (59.7%)

Total Population 9,687,653

Hispanics or Latinos:
- 853,689 people
- 8.8% of the state's population

Hispanics or Latinos may be of any race.

Note: The pie chart shows the racial breakdown of the state's population based on the categories used by the U.S. Bureau of the Census. The Census Bureau reports information for Hispanics or Latinos separately, since they may be of any race. Percentages in the pie chart may not add to 100 because of rounding.

Source: U.S. Bureau of the Census, 2010 Census

After the Civil War, many Georgians moved north, where the industrial revolution was in full swing. In the north, people could find factory work and homes in the growing cities. In Georgia, a small class of industrialists, whose wealth was not dependent on farming, began to arise. But many of Georgia's people, both black and white, struggled to make a living as sharecroppers in the years that followed.

Despite the hardships, the population grew steadily. In 1860, there were just over a million Georgians. By 1900, the number had doubled. At this time, most Georgians lived on farms or in small villages, and 60 percent worked in agriculture, most as tenant farmers.

Sharecroppers in Georgia struggled to support their families.

In the early twentieth century, many young women worked in Georgia's cotton mills.

Few industries came to Georgia from the northeast in the early 1900s. Cotton and lumber mills were established. These mills paid the lowest wages, however, so the poor remained poor while the mill owners stayed rich.

Through the late 1960s, many of Georgia's political leaders prevented the state from progressing socially and extending equal rights and equal opportunity to African American residents. Until January 1961, no African American attended school or college in Georgia with white students. Many Georgians worked long and hard for desegregation to finally happen in the 1960s.

After desegregation, many more people moved to the Southern states and especially to Atlanta, where the city's leaders worked hard to help the African-American community make economic progress. Many of the new residents were the descendants—children, grandchildren, and great-grandchildren—of families that once lived in the South. As a result, the people of Georgia started a new era of progress and opportunity.

Famous Georgians

Juliette Gordon Low: Humanitarian

Born in Savannah in 1860, Low founded the American Girl Scouts in her hometown in 1912. The youth organization stresses good citizenship and service. Activities focus on science, math, technology, physical fitness, the arts, and the outdoors. Low died in 1927, but the Girl Scouts lived on to become a worldwide organization. The World Association of Girl Guides and Girl Scouts reaches 10 million girls in 145 countries.

Ty Cobb: Baseball Player

Many people consider Cobb, born on a farm in Narrows in 1886, to be the greatest baseball player of all time. Playing most of his career with the American League's Detroit Tigers, he compiled a lifetime batting average of .367, the highest in baseball history. In 1911, he led the league in nearly every major offensive category and batted .420. In 1915, he stole 96 bases in 156 games. No one outplayed the man they called the Georgia Peach. Cobb died in 1961.

Margaret Mitchell: Author

Born in Atlanta in 1900, Margaret Mitchell became a reporter for the *Atlanta Journal* newspaper. But her real claim to fame came in 1936, with her novel *Gone with the Wind*. Her romance set during the Civil War period has sold more copies than any other American novel in history. The movie that followed, starring Vivien Leigh and Clark Gable, became another classic. Mitchell died in 1949. Fifty years later, the Associated Press elected her the second-most influential Georgian, after Martin Luther King Jr.

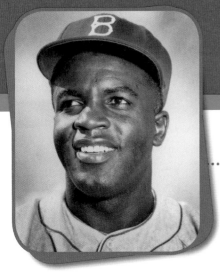

Jackie Robinson: Athlete

Jack Roosevelt Robinson was born in Cairo, Georgia, in 1919. He competed in football, baseball, basketball, and track at the University of California, Los Angeles (UCLA). After three years in the army, he played baseball with the Kansas City Monarchs of the American Negro League in 1945. Later that year—in a historic move that ended decades of discrimination against blacks in baseball—he signed with the Brooklyn Dodgers. After a successful season in 1946 with their farm club, he became, in 1947, the first African American to play in modern Major League Baseball. He died in 1972.

Martin Luther King Jr.: Civil Rights Leader

King was born in Atlanta in 1929. Between 1957 and 1968, King spoke more than 2,500 times, appearing where there was injustice and protest. He was an icon of the civil rights movement. In 1964, at the age of thirty-five, Martin Luther King Jr. won the Nobel Peace Prize. King remains the youngest man to have received this prize. He was assassinated in 1968. Visitors to Washington, D.C., pay their respects to the civil rights leader at the Martin Luther King Jr. Memorial, dedicated in 2011.

Julia Roberts: Actor and Producer

Born in Atlanta in 1967, Julia Roberts moved to Smyrna at age four. Her first major movie role was in *Mystic Pizza*. With *Erin Brockovich*, the true story of a legal assistant who forces a utility company to admit wrongdoing, she won an Academy Award for best actress. Roberts, one of the highest paid actors in the world, is active in supporting charities and humanitarian organizations, such as UNICEF.

Diversity

In the twenty-first century, people of many racial, ethnic, and cultural backgrounds make up the population of Georgia. The number of Hispanic Americans doubled between 2000 and 2010, and Hispanics now make up nearly 9 percent of the population. The growth of the Hispanic population has been especially dramatic in the Atlanta area.

When the Civil War broke out, about half the population of Georgia was African American. In the 1900s, African Americans from the South went north in large numbers. This population shift is called the Great Migration. However, the numbers are shifting back again. The 2010 U.S. Census found that African Americans make up almost one-third of the state's population. The city of Atlanta has become a destination for highly educated black Americans.

Georgia is also experiencing a growth in its other minority

Estimates say that Hispanic Americans will comprise almost one-quarter of Georgia's high school graduates by 2022.

populations. For example, the 2010 Census found that Asian Americans make up about 3 percent of the population. That is one percentage point more than in the 2000 U.S. Census.

New Georgia residents come from around the country and the world. They are drawn to the educational, business, and cultural opportunities that Georgia has to offer. The state educates more than 1.6 million students in kindergarten through grade twelve. There are more than 2,600 schools in approximately 180 districts. The state's fourth graders are outperforming the national average in reading, according to the National Assessment of Educational Progress for 2011.

Georgia's elementary students are thriving in reading, according to national tests.

★ Swamp Gravy, Georgia's Official Folk Life Play

Swamp Gravy, a storytelling tradition, turns music, comedy, and tragedy into unforgettable performances. Local citizens present a new play every year. It is professionally written, designed, directed, and performed each March and October in a seventy-year-old cotton warehouse in Colquitt.

★ St. Patrick's Day

Each March, Savannah holds one of the world's largest St. Patrick's Day events. About a half million people typically attend the parade and enjoy a week of festival activities, located on historic River Street.

★ International Cherry Blossom Festival

In March, Macon welcomes festival lovers to one of the most extravagant displays of springtime color in the nation. This festival celebrates gracious southern hospitality surrounded by the magnificent beauty of more than 300,000 Yoshino cherry trees. Hundreds of events take place during this ten-day festival, including tours of historic homes, musical entertainment, a variety of performances, and exhibits.

★ Georgia Peach Festival

In June, Byron and Fort Valley host the Georgia Peach Festival. This celebration, home to the world's largest peach cobbler, is Georgia's official food fest, with live entertainment, kids' rides, and a parade.

★ Ocmulgee Indian Celebration

In Macon, the many Indian Nations in and around Georgia—including the Creek, Choctaw, Chickasaw, and Cherokee—celebrate their heritage in September. Activities include music, dancing, arts and crafts, storytelling, period encampments, and native food.

★ Savannah Jazz Festival

The internationally celebrated Savannah Jazz Festival, organized by the Coastal Jazz Association, has taken place every year since 1983. Typically held in late September, the festival offers a week of free performances and jam sessions throughout the city.

★ Plains Peanut Festival

In late September, the small town of Plains hosts the peanut festival, complete with free entertainment, historical and educational displays, a 5K run, a recipe contest and tasting, a tractor pull, a rock climbing wall, and much more.

★ Magical Night of Lights

Each year in December, Lake Lanier Islands Resort, near Atlanta, creates the largest display of animated holiday lights in the world. Visitors can drive through 7 miles (11 km) of winter lights displays and visit the Holiday Village, where Santa stays.

★ Oktoberfest

The state's longest Oktoberfest is held in Helen, from the middle of September through the first day of November. This celebration of German culture includes oompah Bavarian music, German food and drinks, and polkas.

How the Government Works

Georgia has 159 counties, more than any other state except Texas. Why does the Peach State have so many counties? Some say that there was a rule of thumb in Georgia that every citizen should live within a half-day trip by horse or wagon from the seat, or center, of the county government.

Every part of Georgia, from the barrier islands to the mountains in the north, falls within a county. Local officials act as an arm of state government, performing many state-related functions, such as holding elections and issuing marriage licenses. Counties also provide a variety of local services to their citizens. However, the way that the counties operate is a local matter. Different types of government exist at the county level. County governments may be headed by a county manager, an administrator, or a commissioner.

The counties are made up of towns, cities, and other communities. Each of these communities has its own government as well. The local officials may be selectmen, mayors, or council members. Local governments handle issues that affect the town or city directly, such as parking regulations.

State Government and Representation in Congress

The state government, with its capital in Atlanta, has three branches. There is a legislature, which passes state laws. The executive branch, headed by the governor, carries out state laws. The judicial branch, which includes the courts,

Georgia's state capitol, located in Atlanta, was built in 1889.

GOVERNOR TURNED PRESIDENT

Jimmy Carter, who has rarely used his full name—James Earl Carter Jr.—was born in Plains in 1924. He served two terms as a state senator and one term as the governor of Georgia, from 1971 to 1975. In 1976, Carter was elected president of the United States, defeating sitting president Gerald Ford. In 1982, he and his wife, Rosalynn, founded Atlanta's Carter Center, which works to advance human rights and ease human suffering. Carter, who won the Nobel Peace Prize in 2002, continues to write, travel on peace missions, and comment on current events.

enforces state laws and can punish people who violate them. The highest court is the supreme court of Georgia. This court can also decide whether state laws agree with the state constitution, which describes the structure, the powers, and the limits on the power of state government.

Georgia elects people to represent the state in both houses of the U.S. Congress in Washington, D.C. Like all states, Georgia sends two senators to the U.S. Senate. The number of members a state sends to the U.S. House of Representatives is based on population. Because the 2010 Census found that Georgia's population had grown significantly in the first decade of the twenty-first century, the state's number of representatives in the House increased from thirteen to fourteen as of 2013.

How a Bill Becomes a Law

The idea for a new law can come from any citizen or group, including students. The idea is shared with a member of the house of representatives or the senate. After the legislator considers the idea, shares it with other legislators, and discusses the legal meaning of the idea with a state attorney, he or she may choose to introduce it as a bill. A bill is a proposed law. When a bill is introduced, it is sent to a committee of legislators for further study and discussion. If the committee approves of the bill, it goes to all the members of the chamber in which it was

Branches of Government

EXECUTIVE ★ ★ ★ ★ ★ ★ ★ ★

The governor is the head of this branch. Voters elect him or her to a four-year term. The governor is limited to two consecutive terms, but a governor who has served two terms and is then out of office for at least four years may run again. The governor proposes to the legislature the state budget and new programs and laws, can veto (reject) legislation, and appoints many state government officials. The governor cannot, however, personally introduce a bill. The executive branch carries out laws and performs such government functions as providing education and maintaining highways. Other members of this branch include the lieutenant governor, attorney general, secretary of state, and superintendent of schools as well as the commissioners of labor, insurance, and agriculture.

LEGISLATIVE ★ ★ ★ ★ ★ ★ ★ ★

The Georgia legislature, which is called the general assembly, is made up of two houses, or chambers. There is a house of representatives, which has 180 members, and a senate, with 56 members. All members of both houses are elected at the same time to two-year terms, and there is no limit on the number of terms a legislator may serve. The legislature has the responsibility of enacting new laws, changing existing laws, and repealing (removing) outdated laws or any other laws it concludes should no longer be in effect. The legislature also approves the annual state budget.

JUDICIAL ★ ★ ★ ★ ★ ★ ★ ★

Georgia's two major courts of appellate jurisdiction are the Georgia court of appeals and the supreme court of Georgia. An appellate court is a court that has the power to review and possibly change the judgment of another court. Georgia's court of appeals has twelve judges. It can hear any appeal from a trial court unless the state constitution directs otherwise. Judges who serve on this court are elected to six-year terms. The supreme court of Georgia has seven justices who make up the state's highest appellate body. They are elected to six-year terms as well. Any appeal that involves the interpretation of the U.S. or Georgia constitution must be heard by the supreme court. Elections for these judges are nonpartisan, which means that candidates do not run as representatives of a political party.

State senators discuss an education bill during a legislative session in Atlanta.

introduced for their consideration. The merits of the bill are debated and amendments (changes) to the bill may be made. Then, the bill is voted on.

If most of the legislators do not agree with the bill and vote against it, the bill may "die," and that idea cannot become a law at that time. If a majority of legislators approve of the bill and vote in favor of it, the bill goes to the other chamber of the legislature for its consideration. There, the bill goes through the same process as in the first chamber. If both chambers vote in favor of, or pass, the bill, it goes to the governor.

If the governor agrees with the bill, he or she can sign it into law. If the governor does not act at all, the bill becomes a law after six days if the general assembly is in session or forty days if it is not in session. If the governor disagrees with the bill, he or she can veto, or reject, it. In many cases, a bill that is vetoed does not become law. However, the legislature can overrule the governor's veto if they have enough votes in support of the bill. To override the governor, both chambers must vote in favor of the bill by a two-thirds majority. If they do, then the bill becomes law despite the governor's objection.

Recently, the legislature has considered a variety of bills, from a ban on texting while driving to a bill that would require drug testing for individuals seeking public assistance. Some bills cover minor issues, such as how meetings are handled. Others address major issues, such as undocumented immigration.

Taking the Lead

Some students in Georgia were able to get an important bill passed that allowed them to raise money to clean a local water source. Their story illustrates democracy in action in Georgia.

The story begins on school property. Storm-water runoff from the school building, parking lot, and sports fields was draining straight into a creek that flows into the Chattahoochee River. This river is the main source of drinking water for Atlanta. The students decided to build a constructed (human-made) wetland, which is a ditch with water and plants usually found in natural wetlands, such as cattails, reeds, and rushes. Such a wetland naturally removes up to 80 percent of pollutants in wastewater passing through it.

The Georgia students persuaded experts to donate a design for the wetland. They also got legislators to help them obtain a grant, or money, for the project. In exchange for the grant, the students had to promote the project to other Georgians. Their state representative suggested offering a reduction of property taxes to any citizen who built and used constructed wetlands on their property. This required that a bill be written and sent before the house and the senate. The bill was approved and became a law. Now, the water of Georgia will be cleaner and safer for everyone.

The Chattahoochee River provides drinking water for the city of Atlanta.

Contacting Lawmakers

★ ★ ★ ★ ★ ★ ★ ★ ★ ★ ★ ★

Citizens of all ages can communicate their concerns and opinions to local and state officials. To find your state legislators go to

http://www.legis.state.ga.us

Click on Find Your Legislator to find information about and photographs of all of Georgia's state representatives and senators.

Making a Living

For many years the Georgia economy was based on cotton production. As the state's businesses branched out, Georgia became known for what are now considered its traditional industries—pulp and paper, food processing, and textiles and carpets. Food-processing plants employ more workers than any other type of manufacturing in Georgia. These plants handle many farm products as well as chickens and other birds raised in the state's large poultry industry. The state's older industries have been supplemented by other areas of business, including aerospace and automotive companies. The Peach State has also been riding the growth in bioscience and high-tech industries. Service businesses such as call centers and firms selling financial products round out the modern Georgia economy.

Agriculture

In former times, agriculture was an adequate description of the food-growing industries in Georgia. These days, the more accurate term is agribusiness. This change better reflects the research and technology that go into large-scale agriculture. This sector of the economy produces $65 billion annually for Georgia. In 2010, the number of farms in the state totaled 47,400. Georgia is generally the nation's top producer of peanuts, broiler chickens, pecans, and watermelons. Other top crops include cotton, peaches, eggs, tobacco, and tomatoes.

Oak trees frame the road on a Savannah plantation. In the past, agriculture contributed greatly to Georgia's economy.

Workers & Industries

Industry	Number of People Working in That Industry	Percentage of All Workers Who Are Working in That Industry
Education and health care	887,000	21.3%
Wholesale and retail businesses	636,133	15.3%
Publishing, media, entertainment, hotels, and restaurants	473,020	11.4%
Professionals, scientists, and managers	457,005	11.0%
Manufacturing	437,159	10.5%
Construction	282,356	6.8%
Banking and finance, insurance, and real estate	257,925	6.2%
Transportation and public utilities	244,713	5.9%
Government	235,729	5.7%
Other services	208,073	5.0%
Farming, fishing, forestry, and mining	46,340	1.1%
Totals	4,165,453	100%

Notes: Figures above do not include people in the armed forces. "Professionals" includes people such as doctors and lawyers.

Source: U.S. Bureau of the Census, 2010 estimates

The boll weevil nearly destroyed the U.S. cotton industry. These insects were wiped out from several states, including Georgia, in the early 1990s. Cotton is now produced on approximately 1.3 million acres (526,000 ha) in the state annually.

Some other insects have been helpful to the economy. The honeybee industry is very important to Georgia. Although this industry has been part of the state's agriculture for only the past century, Georgia is among the leaders in the country's bee production. Honeybee pollination is vital to many of the state's crops, including watermelons, cantaloupes, squash, and tree fruits.

A farmer examines a container of harvested peanuts. Peanut crops are used to produce cooking oil, peanut butter, and snacks.

RECIPE FOR PECAN-CRUSTED PEACH CRISP

This recipe combines Georgia's pecans and peaches for a delicious dessert.

WHAT YOU NEED

Crisp Topping:

1 cup (120 grams) pecan pieces

1 cup (225 g) butter

1 $\frac{1}{4}$ cup (160 g) all-purpose flour

1 cup (200 g) brown sugar

Peaches:

1 cup (225 g) butter

1 cup (200 g) brown sugar

1 teaspoon (0.5 g) cinnamon

4 whole peaches, cut into halves and pitted

Have an adult help you preheat the oven to 350 °F (175 °C). Combine the pecans, 1 cup (225 g) of butter, the flour, and 1 cup (200 g) of brown sugar in a bowl until the mixture is crumbly.

Place the mixture on a sheet pan and, with adult help, bake it in the preheated oven until crisp. Set aside the baked mixture.

Combine the rest of the butter, the brown sugar, and the cinnamon in a saucepan, and cook over low heat until the butter is melted. Add the peaches, and cook until they are tender and a syrup forms.

Put the peach halves and syrup into serving bowls and cover with your pecan crisp topping. You can serve with ice cream or whipped cream. Enjoy!

Some of the biggest challenges facing Georgia's farmers involve national agricultural issues. The shift toward factory-like farming controlled by fewer and fewer companies is impacting small farms and rural communities. These shifts have a negative effect on the biodiversity, or variety, of plants and livestock. In addition, the chemicals used to fertilize

crops, to kill insects that damage crops, and to control diseases among farm animals can pollute the environment and find their way into human diets. A growing group of farmers in Georgia is moving toward organic farming as a way of providing safe, healthful, and nutritious food choices. They are finding that organic farming can also improve farm family incomes and protect natural resources.

Poultry

Of all the states, Georgia ranks first in poultry production. Poultry producers turn out 24.6 million pounds (11.2 million kg) of chicken and 14 million eggs each day, on average. The poultry industry's yearly contribution to the state's economy is now more than $13 billion. Of course, all those chickens produce billions of pounds (kilograms) of waste per year. Some of the manure washes into waterways that supply drinking water. The manure pollutes rivers and lakes with hormones and bacteria that can cause illness, and with phosphorus, which causes algae blooms. The algae blooms then kill fish by reducing oxygen levels in the water.

A program sponsored by the University of Georgia has been teaching farmers how to manage the chicken litter. Options include reusing and recycling it. "The whole purpose of the plan is to teach farmers how to apply chicken litter correctly to soil as a fertilizer and avoid . . . contamination in soil and groundwater," poultry scientist Dan Cunningham has said.

Products & Resources

Pulp and Paper

Georgia is home to more than twenty pulp and paper mills that produce more paper and paperboard than any state except Alabama. Georgia's mills send $10 billion of pulp and paperboard products around the world.

Peanuts

Africans introduced peanuts to North America. Today, Georgia produces about 45 percent of the total U.S. peanut crop. More than half the state's peanuts are used to make peanut butter. The Georgia general assembly selected the peanut as the official state crop in 1995.

Peaches

A Peach County schoolteacher once asked her class to identify the four seasons of the year. The response that she received was fall, winter, spring—and peach season. Georgia is known as the Peach State because of its reputation for producing the highest-quality fruit. The peach became the official state fruit in 1995.

Shrimp

Available in supermarkets and, along the Atlantic coast, at roadside fish markets, Georgia shrimp are appreciated by many seafood lovers. Georgia's rich marshlands are relatively unpolluted, and they produce an abundance of shrimp that are especially tender, sweet, and meaty. Many people consider these shrimp to be the best in the world.

Pecans

Long before Europeans arrived in Georgia, American Indians were enjoying the pecans that grew wild in the area. Pecan production is centered in Albany-Dougherty County, in the area known as the Pecan Capital of the World. Georgia farmers produce about 85 million pounds (38 million kg) of pecans a year.

Transportation Equipment

Georgia produces aircraft parts, automobiles, and military aircraft and missiles. Manufacturers of aerospace equipment with a presence in Georgia include Boeing, Cessna, Gulfstream, and Lockheed Martin. The state exports more than $2 billion in autos and related parts. The state is also home to the country's largest manufacturer of school buses, the Big Bird Corporation.

Kia Motors officials take part in a groundbreaking ceremony for a new manufacturing plant in West Point.

Manufacturing

Some of the largest manufacturers in Georgia are Kia Motors, the automobile producer headquartered in Seoul, South Korea, and the aerospace and aircraft company Lockheed Martin. About 11 percent of the annual economy is related to manufacturing industries, including food processing. Tyson Foods is one of the largest employers in the state. International Paper is another one of the largest companies, as is Shaw Industries, which makes carpet, tile, and other flooring. Some of the newest manufacturers to open for business in Georgia include makers of recycled glass surfaces, specialty chemicals, and bed pillows. Manufacturers of solar and wind energy products, such as solar panels and wind turbine components, have also recently entered the state.

Armed Services

The American military is one of Georgia's largest employers. Fort Stewart, Robins Air Force Base, Fort McPherson, Hunter Army Air Field, Fort Gordon, Moody Air Force Base, Kings Bay Naval Submarine Base, the Naval Air Station at Atlanta, and Fort Benning employ thousands of people.

Not only humans work for the military. Georgia's Fort Benning is a training ground for military working dogs. War dogs are credited with saving the lives of tens of thousands of soldiers dating back to World War II. German shepherds and Labrador retrievers are the most popular dogs used in combat because of their excellent temperaments, intelligence, and senses of smell, sight, and hearing. The U.S. Department of Homeland Security and various police forces also use many of Benning's canine "graduates."

Georgia Works

Ever since the port of Savannah was founded and Atlanta was settled around a railroad terminal, Georgia has been an important transportation center. Today, Hartsfield-Jackson Atlanta International Airport is one of the busiest, if not the busiest, passenger airports in the world. Delta Air Lines is one of Georgia's larger employers. Lockheed Martin Aeronautics in Marietta builds military aircraft and employs thousands of Georgians.

As in most states in modern America, the largest portion of the work force in Georgia is employed in service industries. Many Georgians work for wholesale businesses, which sell goods in large quantities to retailers, or in retail businesses, which sell products directly to consumers.

Many other Georgians are employed in service industries such as health care, education, law, and data processing. Large numbers also work in finance, insurance, and banking, as well as in real estate.

Nearly 90 million passengers use Hartsfield-Jackson Atlanta International Airport each year.

Turner Field, the home of the Braves, opened in 1997.

An enormous number of people travel to Georgia for business and leisure every year. Tourism is a major part of the service sector of the economy. Museum staff, tour guides, servers at restaurants, and hotel workers earn money through Georgia tourism.

With so much to offer, it is no wonder that the Peach State continues to attract visitors and new residents. There are thirty-seven universities and colleges in the Georgia University System, including the University of Georgia, in Athens, and Georgia State, in Atlanta. The Georgia Sports Hall of Fame, in Macon, is the largest sports hall in the nation. Fans root for Atlanta-based professional teams that include the Falcons in the National Football League, the Hawks in the National Basketball Association, the Braves in Major League Baseball's National League, and the Thrashers in the National Hockey League.

Atlanta is home to the Callanwolde Fine Arts Center, known for arts education, along with the High Museum of Art and numerous other museums. In the northern part of the state, the ArtWorks Artisan Centre showcases handicrafts. There is the Musical Theatre Festival on Jekyll Island in the east. The Columbus Symphony performs in the south. In each region, for every season, there is a wealth of culture and entertainment to enjoy in Georgia.

State Flag & Seal

On May 8, 2003, the governor of Georgia signed a bill creating a new state flag for the state. The flag consists of a field of three horizontal bars of equal width, two red bars separated by a white bar in the center. In the upper left corner is a square blue area the width of two bars. In the center of the blue area is a circle of thirteen white stars, symbolizing Georgia and the other twelve original states. Within the circle of stars is Georgia's coat of arms immediately above the words In God We Trust—both in gold.

The Great Seal of Georgia was adopted in 1798. On its front side appear three pillars supporting an arch, representing the three branches of government—legislative, judicial, and executive. A militiaman stands with a drawn sword defending the state constitution, whose principles are wisdom, justice, and moderation. Circling the image are the words State of Georgia and the year 1776, to commemorate the signing of the Declaration of Independence.

GEORGIA

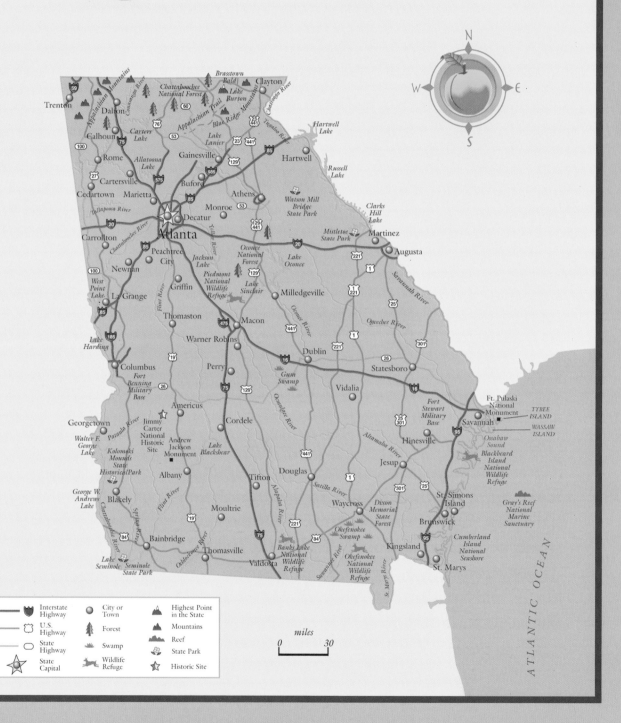

Map Legend:

- Interstate Highway
- U.S. Highway
- State Highway
- State Capital
- City or Town
- Forest
- Swamp
- Wildlife Refuge
- Highest Point in the State
- Mountains
- Reef
- State Park
- Historic Site

miles
0   30

Labels on map:

Trenton, Dalton, Calhoun, Rome, Cartersville, Cedartown, Marietta, Buford, Gainesville, Clayton, Hartwell, Athens, Monroe, Decatur, Atlanta, Carrollton, Peachtree City, Newnan, Griffin, La Grange, Thomaston, Warner Robins, Macon, Perry, Columbus, Americus, Cordele, Georgetown, Albany, Blakely, Moultrie, Bainbridge, Thomasville, Valdosta, Tifton, Douglas, Waycross, Kingsland, St. Marys, Brunswick, St. Simons Island, Jesup, Hinesville, Savannah, Statesboro, Vidalia, Dublin, Milledgeville, Martinez, Augusta, Hartwell

Appalachian Mountains, Coosawattee River, Chattahoochee National Forest, Brasstown Bald, Lake Burton, Appalachian Trail, Blue Ridge Mountains, Chattooga River, Tugaloo River, Hartwell Lake, Carters Lake, Lake Lanier, Allatoona Lake, Russell Lake, Clarks Hill Lake, Watson Mill Bridge State Park, Mistletoe State Park, Tallapoosa River, Chattahoochee River, Yellow River, Oconee National Forest, Lake Oconee, Savannah River, West Point Lake, Jackson Lake, Piedmont National Wildlife Refuge, Lake Sinclair, Oconee River, Ogeechee River, Flint River, Lake Harding, Fort Benning Military Base, Gum Swamp, Ocmulgee River, Fort Stewart Military Base, Ft. Pulaski National Monument, Tybee Island, Wassaw Island, Ossabaw Sound, Blackbeard Island National Wildlife Refuge, Walter F. George Lake, Pataula Creek, Jimmy Carter National Historic Site, Andrew Jackson Monument, Kolomoki Mounds State Historical Park, Lake Blackshear, Altamaha River, Gray's Reef National Marine Sanctuary, George W. Andrews Lake, Chattahoochee River, Flint River, Spring Creek, Satilla River, Dixon Memorial State Forest, Cumberland Island National Seashore, Lake Seminole, Seminole State Park, Oolockonee River, Alapaha River, Banks Lake National Wildlife Refuge, Withlacoochee River, Okefenokee Swamp, Okefenokee National Wildlife Refuge, St. Marys River, ATLANTIC OCEAN

State Song

Georgia on My Mind

words by Stuart Gorrell
music by Hoagy Carmichael

CHORUS

that's where I be - long. Geor-gia, _ Geor-gia, _ the whole day through. Just an

old sweet song keeps GEOR-GIA ON MY MIND *(Geor-gia on my mind).* Geor-gia, _ Geor-gia, _

a song of you Comes as sweet and clear as moon-light through the pines. _____

BOOKS

Bader, Bonnie. *Who Was Martin Luther King, Jr.?* New York: Grosset & Dunlap, 2008.

Jerome, Kate Boehm. *Savannah and the State of Georgia: Cool Stuff Every Kid Should Know.* Charleston, SC: Arcadia Publishing, 2011.

Kent, Deborah. *The Trail of Tears.* Danbury, CT: Children's Press, 2007.

Osborne, Linda Barrett. *Traveling the Freedom Road: From Slavery and the Civil War Through Reconstruction.* New York: Abrams Books for Young Readers, 2009.

Raum, Elizabeth. *Gift of Peace: The Jimmy Carter Story.* Grand Rapids, MI: Zonderkidz, 2011.

WEBSITES

Georgia Department of Economic Development Website:
http://www.exploregeorgia.org

Georgia Secretary of State Website:
http://www.sos.georgia.gov

Georgia's State Government Website:
http://www.georgia.gov

Karen Diane Haywood has edited many books for young people. She lives in North Carolina, where she watches the squirrels steal fruit from the apple trees in her backyard.

Jessica Cohn has worked in educational publishing for more than a decade, writing and editing articles and books. She lives in New York State. Her last trip to Georgia included explorations of the welcoming cities of Atlanta and Athens.

Page numbers in **boldface** are illustrations.